GREECE

GREECE

Emma Howard

CHARTWELL
BOOKS, INC.

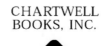

Published in 2009 by Compendium Publishing,
43 Frith Street, London W1D 4SA, United Kingdom.

CHARTWELL BOOKS, INC.
A Division of
BOOK SALES, INC.
276 Fifth Avenue Suite 206
New York, New York 10001

ISBN 13: 978-0-7858-2531-9
ISBN 10: 0-7858-2531-2

Design: Ian Welch/Peran Publishing Services

All Internet site information provided was correct when provided by the Author. The Publisher can accept no responsibility for this information becoming incorrect.

Printed in China through Printworks Int. Ltd.

PAGE 1: A small church in Aegina, one of the Sarconic Islands, named after the mother of Aeacus, who was born in and ruled the island.
via Jo St. Mart

PAGE 2: The Acropolis rises 150 m (490 ft) above sea level and overlooks the city of Athens.
via Jo St. Mart

PAGES 4-5: The Corinth Canal was built in the late 19th Century and connects the Gulf of Corinth with the Saronic Gulf in the Aegean Sea.
via Jo St. Mart

OVER PAGE: The old town of Chania—situated next to the old harbor—in western Crete was surrounded by Venetian fortifications that were built from 1538.
Simon Plant/zefa/Corbis/42-16186038

Contents

Introduction

Introduction

Greece is steeped in an illustrious history. At various points in its past, it has been a powerhouse of political, social, artistic, and scientific discovery. A relatively small nation, Greece has been the birthplace of people and ideas that have changed the world.

Situated between Europe, Asia, and Africa on the edge of the Balkan Peninsula, it is a country covered in steep mountains, deep ravines, idyllic fishing villages, dynamic cities, and surrounded by thousands of sun kissed islands. Human settlements of the area began as early as 4500 B.C. and the earliest recorded civilization was that of the Minoans, a remarkably advanced society located on the island of Crete. By 3000 B.C., the Minoans had founded a successful culture based on trade, built magnificent palaces, and proved themselves masterful in the fields of art, sculpture, jewelry, and pottery. In fact, they were so successful that they dominated the area around the Aegean for almost 2,000 years and such was their influence that the burgeoning society of the mainland, the Mycenaeans, adopted much of their culture. The latter blossomed under the guidance of their island neighbors, so much so that by 1450 B.C. they took control of Crete and went on to form an empire that included Sicily, sections of southern Italy and Asia, and the Levant Coast. There followed a period of great prosperity for these early Greeks and many impressive monuments were erected all over the mainland. One of the most well-known and well preserved edifices of this period in Greek history is the Lion Gate at Mycenae.

Unfortunately, in the middle of the 12th Century a catastrophic event destroyed the entire Mycenaean culture. The great buildings were destroyed or left abandoned and the settlements were deserted. Nobody knows for sure what caused such an advanced and strong culture to virtually disappear overnight. Historians speculate a massive natural disaster might have occurred, some suggest that over-enthusiastic deforestation could have

RIGHT: Mount Lycabettus, a Cretaceous limestone hill, rises above Athens and is home to the 19th Century Chapel of St George, a theatre and a restaurant.
via Jo St. Mart

disrupted the economy. We will probably never know, as there are no records from the time and Greece then entered a kind of Dark Age, when overseas trade and even the art of writing seems to have died out completely. During this dark time in history, evidence suggests that the remaining people moved to smaller settlements closer to the sea.

No reliable records become available until the year 776 B.C.. In this year, at a small *polis* called Elis, the first Olympic Games were held. According to reports all the local athletes competed well and won many events. It was a spectacle that would become a regular occurrence over the following centuries.

During the 8th Century B.C., the country was split into a number of self ruling and rival city states, each controlled by a noble. Every city was laid out in roughly the same way with a citadel (or *acropolis*) at the centre, a market square surrounded by homes for the nobles, soldiers, and merchants, and a fortified wall along the outside for protection. The farmers and slaves would live and work on the land surrounding this defensive barrier. Due to the country's mostly barren landscape and shortage of viable farmland, quarrels over boundaries were frequent and sometimes bloody. In order to stop unnecessary bloodshed the rulers became adept at political machinations, forging alliances, and deception.

In the 7th Century B.C., a massive change took place in the Greek military, which would go on to have a profound effect on the country for years to come. For centuries war had been fought in the same way, with individual fighters hacking and slashing at the enemy on a confused and chaotic battlefield. All this was to change with the innovation of the *phalanx*. Consisting of a group of heavily armed men, each holding a shield, spear, and a sword, the soldiers stood close together with their shields protecting the sword arm of their neighbor. In doing this they formed an almost impenetrable screen against attackers. The arrangement of the phalanx fostered deep loyalty and trust between the soldiers, who fought fiercely to defend their neighboring fighter because if one were to fall then the others would be vulnerable. The most famous of all the Greek fighters were undoubtedly the Spartans, whose names conjure up an image of fearless and valiant warriors even today.

At this time the two most powerful of these city states were Athens and Sparta, but it was not long before Athens became the more prominent of the two. Throughout the course of the 6th Century B.C., Athens grew in size and wealth. It boasted many fine buildings and temples. A massive plaza was built, replacing the smaller market square, which became the focal point for the city. Here the people of Athens could buy, sell, meet, listen to religious or political debate or watch the theater. In fact, the only part of Athenean life that remained unchanged was the difficult political situation. Still suffering from the bitter feuds between rival clans, the country could not move forward for fear of being stabbed in the back. All this would soon change thanks

to one visionary—a man named Cleisthenes. Realizing that much of the problem stemmed from peoples loyalties to their clan or ruling nobleman—rather than their country or their city—he suggested that each free man could vote for one man from their town to represent them (and their interests) in an assembly. Taking its name from the Greek *demos* (meaning people) and *kratos* (meaning rule), the first democratic state was born in 507 B.C.. It would later become the template for modern politics. These changes gave the everyday men of Athens the chance to feel part of something greater than mere family or clan. They now had the rights of citizenship, something that would foster a fierce and patriotic pride. This passion would soon be vital for the future of the country as a mighty enemy rose in the east.

For decades the Persian Empire had been relentlessly conquering and subjugating country after country and it was not long before the colossal nation turned its eyes westward. Slowly Persia moved forward, taking several of the Greek city-states on the Asian continent under their command. But rather than bow to Persian dominion, the Greeks rebelled. Athens sent ships to help the resistance though the larger Persian army, led by King Darius I, quickly quelled the rebellion. Infuriated by the Athenian gall in supplying ships, Darius decided to take the mainland and crush such interfering upstarts under the heel of the superior Persian forces.

Unfortunately for Darius, he had underestimated just how fiercely the men of Athens were prepared fight in order to retain their freedom. He also misjudged how ruthlessly efficient Athenian soldiers could be. The two sides met on the Plains of Marathon in 490 B.C. and the Persian aggressors were quickly defeated. The victorious Athenian army marched back to the capital where the Persian fleet was about to land, expecting to find a cowed and beaten opponent. Instead they found a jubilant enemy army ready to fight again and the fleet immediately fled. Persia tried once more to conquer Greece, but again were beaten back thanks in no small part to the valiant efforts of King Leonidas of Sparta and his famous 300 troops. The tale of the small band of brave, yet ultimately doomed, Spartans taking on the full force of the Persian army has become the stuff of legend.

Now the threat conquest had gone, problems between the city-states began to rise—the two principal rivals being Athens and Sparta. Civil war raged from 431 to 404 B.C., with Sparta eventually victorious. Their rule, however, was cut short by the arrival of King Phillip II of Macedonia. He marched through the country in 353 B.C. and united the country under his rule. When Phillip died in 336 B.C., it was left to his son, Alexander, to take the reins of leadership—something he did with ease. Alexander the Great, as he became known, would go on to conquer Persia, stretching his empire as far east as India and south to Egypt. By the time Alexander died in 323 B.C., Greek culture had spread across Europe and parts of Asia.

With the loss of Alexander, a new power began to spread from the west. The Romans' military

supremacy was overwhelming and by 146 B.C. they had taken control of Macedonia, with Greece falling twenty years later. The relationship between the Greeks and Romans was a complicated one, much more than that of most conquerors and the conquered. Greek cities had been present in Italy for centuries and the culture of Greece had permeated into Roman society. The Romans respected the Greeks and admired their ideals. In fact, under Roman rule the country flourished. They benefited from new roads and buildings and, more importantly, the esteem of Rome. Now that the city-states no longer fought between themselves, Greece built on their existing reputation as a leader in the realms of science and philosophy. In religion, too, Greece was open to new ideas. In 51 A.D., the apostle Paul came to Corinth and began preaching the ways of Christianity. Relatively soon after the gods of ancient Greece were abandoned and replaced with the teachings of Jesus.

When the Roman Empire fell in 395 A.D., Greece became part of the East Roman Empire, later known as the Byzantine Empire, but despite being part of a larger whole, suffered constant attacks from neighboring countries. Each time, though, the might of the Byzantine Empire repelled the invaders. By 750 A.D., the country was enjoying a period of relative peace. It was not destined to last.

At the end of the 9th Century, the Bulgars, under the rule of Simeon I, tried again and again to take Greece. For the next hundred years war raged on. Each time the invaders gained a foothold, they would be beaten back, only to return again. It was not until the beginning of the 11th Century that the Byzantine Empire was finally victorious. Bulgaria was defeated and now that it was part of the empire, it acted as a barrier to any other invading forces. Greece could once again breathe a collective sigh of relief now that immediate threats were extinguished.

It was not until 1145 and the beginning of the Second Crusade, that Greece would be plundered once more. Much of the country was divided between the crusaders, including the Normans and the Sicilians until 1261 when Michael VIII managed to wrest much of the country from the hands of invaders and back into the Byzantine Empire.

Unfortunately a much bigger threat was making its presence felt to the east. The Ottoman Empire began attacking all the Byzantine territories, including Greece, without mercy. Struggling against such an enormous foe, the empire crumbled and by 1460 almost all of Greece was in Ottoman hands. Only the mountains in the west provided any safe haven for the Greeks as the invaders found them difficult to capture. Crete was still owned by Venice. This was a difficult time for the Greek people as the invaders were harsh rulers. Not only were the people reduced to the level of servants to the Ottoman aristocracy, but they were heavily taxed and all non-Muslim Greeks were forced to give up one male child out of every five to join the Ottoman army and be raised as a Muslim. Many fled to the mountains to avoid the demands of the new rulers, others went to Europe, but many stayed and suffered under the new regime.

In 1789 the people of Greece were inspired by the example of the French Revolution and later were overjoyed when Napoleon Bonaparte defeated Venice in 1797 and handed the Ionian Islands back to the people, granting them autonomous rule. For the first time since the Ottomans seized power, the people of Greece harbored dreams of their long lost democracy. The overwhelming desire for freedom came to a head on March 25, 1821, when their fight for independence began in earnest. The Ottomans took heavy losses during the initial days, but soon rallied their forces and took pitiless retribution on the rebels. The world watched as the Ottomans committed terrible atrocities on the Greek people, but did not intervene until 1827 when British, Russian, and French troops sank the Ottoman fleet. Following the famous victory, the allies orchestrated Greek independence in the form of a monarchy. King Otto was brought in from Bavaria and ruled until 1863, when he was deposed and Prince Vilhelm of Denmark took the throne.

The 20th Century brought little in the way of peace for the Greek people. The Balkan Wars of 1912–13 saw many territories won back from the Ottoman Empire, including Crete, Samos, Epirus, and Southern Macedonia. When the First World War began, Greece fought valiantly against Germany, Austria, and the Ottoman Empire, but this led directly into another skirmish with the remnants of the empire. The Greco–Turkish

RIGHT: Samos City from the sea. The island was the birthplace of the Greek scholar Pythagoras.
via Jo St. Martvia Jo St. Mart

War (1919–22) resulted in thousands of Greek Muslims being expelled from Greece and a million Greeks were thrown out of Turkey.

The Second World War saw the country occupied by German forces, but the indomitable spirit of the Greek resistance was instrumental in the Allied victory. The resistance managed to delay German troops in their attempts to invade Russia, resulting in a disastrous march into the jaws of a harsh Russian winter. This effectively ended Germany's chances of winning the war.

After so long spent fighting, Greece's economy was in ruins and the country was caught in a bitter civil war, fighting the onslaught of communism. Peace eventually descended in 1949. Finally, the country could take stock and begin to rebuild. The burgeoning tourist trade added to the country's wealth during the 1960s and 1970s, as did the Marshall Plan. The Greek military came to power after a successful coup, aided in no small part by the CIA. This state of affairs would not last, however, and in the mid-1970s military control over the country collapsed following the Athens Polytechnic uprising in 1973 and the invasion of Cyprus by the Turks in 1974. Finally in 1975, and after the deposing of King Constantine II, Greece was able to implement a truly democratic republican constitution and reclaim the self-determination that had been lost to them for so many years.

Now the country is flourishing. Massive tourist and shipping industries are helping the country improve significantly, giving its people a vastly enhanced standard of living. Greece was one of the first countries to enter the EU (they joined in 1981) and was also quick to embrace the Euro (adopted as the new form of currency in 2002). They have buried the hatchet with old enemy (and close neighbour) Turkey, fully supporting their bid to join the EU.

Life for the Greek people has taken a turn for the better after so many years of upheaval. Millions of people travel to the mainland to see the ancient treasures of Athens or bask on the idyllic islands dotted around the coast. Now the Greek people can sit back and enjoy the many natural splendors their country has to offer in the knowledge that such a jewel was worth the fight and the wait.

RIGHT: The picturesque scenery off the coast of Crete, the largest of the Greek islands and the fifth largest island in the Mediterranean Sea. *KaYann/Fotolia*

RIGHT AND FAR RIGHT: These two views of the Erechtheum show the temple on the north side of the Acropolis in Athens as it was in the latter half of the 19th Century and as it is in the 21st Century. *Library of Congress and via Jo St. Mart*

FAR LEFT, LEFT AND OVER PAGE: With its myriad of beautiful beaches, clear blue seas, inviting cuisine and archaeological treasures, Greece is perhaps Europe's most popular tourist destination.
Ellen Rooney/Robert Harding World Imagery/Corbis, Angelo Cavalli/Robert Harding World Imagery/Corbis and Ljupco Smokovski/Fotolia

FAR LEFT: A colorful evening scene in Santorini, a small, circular archipelago of volcanic islands located in the southern Aegean Sea.
Argonautis/Fotolia

LEFT: The head of a warrior on the East Pediment Sculpture from the Temple of Aphaia in Aegina. Part of the eastern pediment was destroyed during the Persian Wars.
Ljupco Smokovski/Fotolia

RIGHT AND FAR RIGHT: An old dream was finally realized at the end of the 19th Century when the Corinth Canal was opened through isthmus. The first picture dates from around 1906 while the car and train bridges can clearly be seen in the more recent image.
Library of Congress and Vangelis Thomaidis/Fotolia

RIGHT: Between 95% and 98% of all Greeks belong to the Greek Orthodox church. Here is one of the many religious ceremonies held in Athens.
Charles & Josette Lenars/Corbis

FAR RIGHT: The ancestral home of the Olympic Games, Athens has twice hosted the modern Summer Olympics; in 1896 and 2004.
John Harper/Corbis

OVER PAGE: The port of Livadi at dusk. Located in the Larissa prefecture in the periphery of Thessaly, this region became part of Greece between 1881 and 1913.
Atlantide Phototravel/Corbis

Mainland and Coast

Mainland and Coast

Greece has the tenth longest coastline in the world (approximately 9,500 miles) and thousands of islands scattered across its seas. For years, the splendor of its beaches and laid-back coastal towns have attracted tourists from all across the globe. The Peloponnese, a large peninsula joined to the Greek mainland at the Isthmus of Corinth and the Rio-Antirio bridge, boasts a wealth of historic towns and cities alongside a tranquil sea-side existence. The Isthmus of Corinth, the small land bridge joining the mainland to the Peloponnese, was severed in two by the completion of the Corinth Canal in 1893, but before then rulers throughout history had tried and failed to carve a path through the isthmus. In the 7th century B.C., it was the tyrannical ruler Periander who first endeavored to build a canal, but found the task too difficult and gave up. The ancient Romans were the next to make an attempt in 32 A.D. under Emperor Tiberius. Due to insufficient equipment, this effort also failed. Finally, in 67 A.D., Emperor Nero commanded 6,000 slaves equipped with shovels and ordered the completion of a canal. Perhaps fortunately for the slaves, Nero died the following year and the project was cancelled. Nowadays travellers to the coastal regions of Greece are more likely to build sandcastles on the many white sandy beaches that Greece has to offer.

RIGHT AND FAR RIGHT: The location may be the same but the style of nautical vessel in Piraeus harbor has changed dramatically from the latter half of the 19th Century.
Library of Congress and via Jo St. Mart

LEFT: The town of Vathia in Laconia, on the Mani peninsula, attracts tourists by the coachload in spring because of the wild flowers that cover the breathtaking views of the nearby hills.
Schmitz-Söhnigen/zefa/Corbis

RIGHT: The fortress of Bourtzi can be seen from the palm tree-lined waterfront promenade in Nafplion, Greece.
Paul A. Souders/Corbis

RIGHT: The marina at Kalamata, the second-largest city of the Peloponnese. The capital and chief port of the Messenia prefecture, it lies along the Nedon River at the head of the Messenian Gulf.
Andreas G. Karelias/fotoLibra

FAR RIGHT: A Turkish octagonal tower—the Bourtzi—guards the entrance to Methoni. The medieval port was the Venetians' first, and longest-held, possession in the Peloponnese.
Nicholas Kinson/fotoLibra

FAR LEFT: The country's first capital from 1829 until 1834, Nafplio boasts elegant Venetian mansions, neo-classical mansions and intriguing narrow streets.
Nadia Isakova/fotoLibra

LEFT: A sidewalk cafe at Hotel Grande Bretagne in Nauplia near the north end of the Argolic Gulf. The majority of the old town is situated on a peninsula but urban spread has reached the surrounding hillsides.
Richard T. Nowitz/Corbis

FAR LEFT: The caves in Perama are among the most spectacular in Greece. They house a multitude of stalactites and stalagmites that fascinate tourists.
David Walton/fotoLibra

LEFT: A spectacular sunset with the Patras lighthouse overlooking the Gulf of Patraikos and hills of northern Greece at dusk.
Rachel Royse/Corbis

OVER PAGE: Lixouri is the second-largest town on Kefalonia. The largest of the Ionian Islands, Kefalonia is remembered as the setting for the novel *Captain Corelli's Mandolin*.
via Jo St. Mart

Islands

Islands

Scattered throughout the glittering waters surrounding the mainland of Greece are no fewer than 2,000 islands. Grouped under the titles of the Cyclades, the North Aegean islands, the Dodecanese, the Ionian islands, the Sporades, and the Argo-Saronic islands, only 170 are inhabited and some are more famous than others, but each has a unique geography and a few can boast a lasting place in history. Crete, for example, measuring 3,219 square miles is the fifth largest island in the Mediterranean Sea, but was the birthplace of Europe's oldest civilisation, the Minoans, named after the famed King Minos. Settlements date back as far as 3000 B.C. and tales of the Minoan's legendary adventures and heroes were immortalized by Homer in his works the *Iliad* and the *Odyssey*. The Minoans were one of the first people to form a civilization based on trade and evidence of their skills in building, art, jewelry, and sculpture remain to this day in museums around the globe. Yet Crete is not the only island that can boast an permanent place in the annals of history. Rhodes was once home to one of the seven wonders of the world—the Colossus of Rhodes. Now lost to antiquity, the colossus was a statue of Helios, the ancient Greek god of the sun, and stood astride the port of Rhodes. It is estimated to have measured 30 meters in height.

Corfu, the second largest of the Ionian Islands, has a place in mythology as the honeymoon spot for Poseidon and his new wife Korkyra. He allowed her to name the island after herself and when their son Phaiax was born, the surrounding islanders were called the Phaiakes. As time passed the names would evolve into the names we recognize today; Corfu and the Phaeanians.

RIGHT: The picturesque harbor area of Agios Nikolaos in Crete. Located on the eastern part of the island on the bay of Mirabello, the capital of Lassithi prefecture retains its old world charm. *Creasource/Corbis*

FAR LEFT: Spinalonga Island's fortress was built in 1579 by the Venetians to protect Elounda Bay and the Gulf of Mirabello.
Phil Jones/fotoLibra

LEFT: On the north coast of the island of Crete lies the ancient port of Rethymnon. Now a popular and lively tourist center, the town is alive with delightful bars and restaurants.
Peter Adams/Corbis

LEFT: Fishing boats line the marina of a small fishing town on the rocky coastline of Hydra. The island is ringed with wonderful beaches, some sandy, some stony, but all characterized by crystal clear blue waters.
Roman Soumar/Corbis

OVER PAGE: Sunbathers at Shipwreck Beach—officially named Navagio Beach but also known as Smugglers Cove—on Zakynthos Island. Smugglers being pursued by the Greek Navy hit rocks before being washed ashore in 1983.
Atlantide Phototravel/Corbis

ABOVE: Boats moored in the port of Hydra Town. The buildings here are unique. Called Manors, these huge houses were constructed during the island's economic boom of the late 18th Century. Stone-built, flat-roofed, and three or four storys tall, they contain large airy high-ceilinged rooms with distinctive decoration and furniture. *Jon Hicks/Corbis*

LEFT: A fisherman proudly shows off his catch on the quayside in Hydra. Now a quiet but sought after destination, Hydra in the 1950s became a popular colony for artists, musicians, and film makers and remains an artists' destination. The town is built like an amphitheater around the port and it retains an air of romance, in part because no wheeled vehicles are allowed into town. Instead everything, including people, are transported by donkey.
Annebicque Bernard/Corbis Sygma

RIGHT: A fisherman mends his colorful nets on Samos. Situated in the northeast Aegean Sea just off the coast of Asia Minor, this mountainous island was home to the philosopher, mathematician, and musician Pythagoras (580–500 B.C.). Locals claim that his spirit still inhabits Mt. Kerkis, the highest point on Samos, and appears as a light at the peak to guide fishermen safely home during storms.
Michael Boys/Corbis

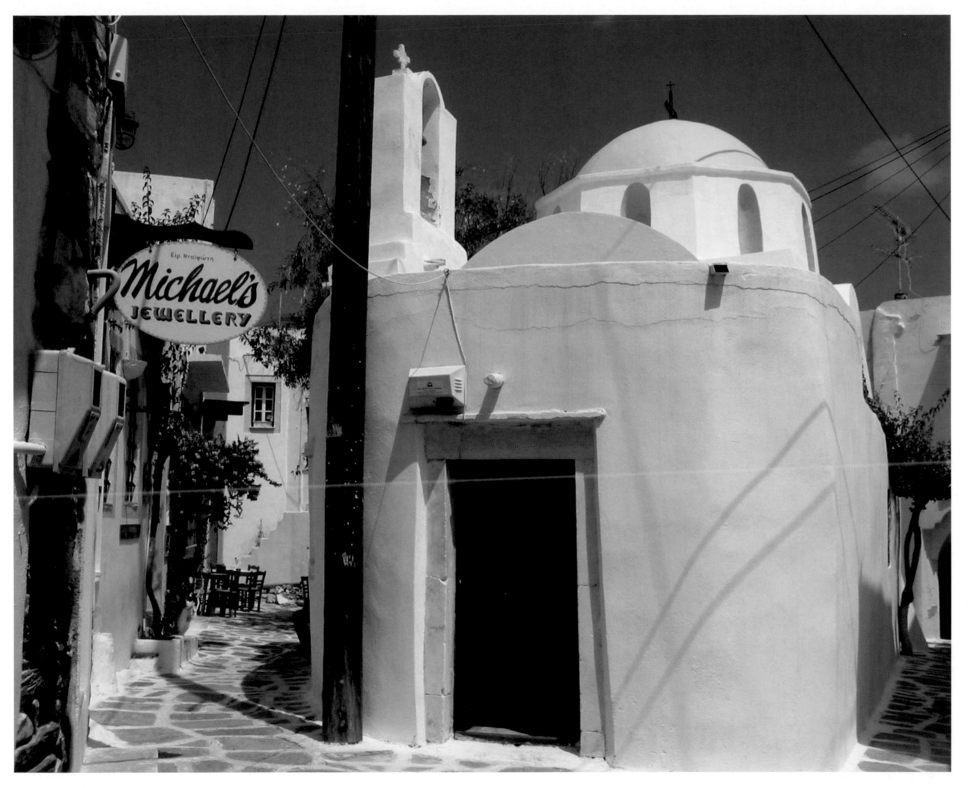

FAR LEFT: Poros is a small island in the Saronic Gulf, separated from the Peloponnese by only a couple of hundred meters. The pretty clocktower was built in 1927.
via Jo St. Mart

LEFT: Naoussa on Paros is considered by many to be one of the prettiest villages in the Cyclades. The whitewashed buildings surround the port in a wandering maze of narrow stone-paved streets, all overlooked by the ruins of a Venetian castle perched on the hill above. The highest spot in the village itself is occupied by the church of Agios Nikolaos, now a museum containing Byzantine artifacts and valuable 13th Century icons.
via Jo St. Mart

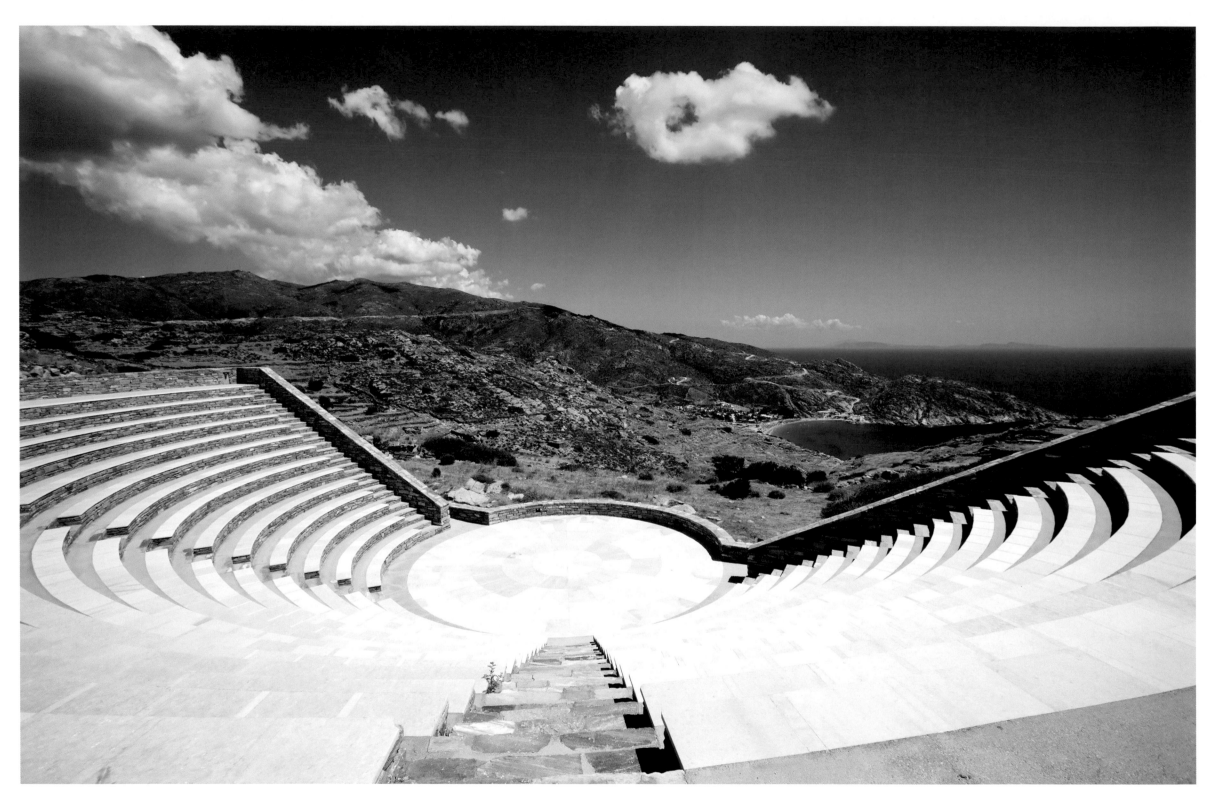

FAR LEFT: The Odysseas Elytis open air theater on the island of Ios was named after the Greek poet who was awarded the Nobel Prize in Literature in 1979.
Alex Yeung/Fotolia

LEFT: St Paul's Bay on Rhodes. It was in this idyllic spot that the apostle landed in 58 A.D.
Stephen Mcadam/fotoLibra

OVER PAGE: Located only 26 kilometers from the city of Rhodes, on the eastern coast of the Rhodes Island, the breathtaking beauty of Tsambika Beach is obvious.
Atlantide Phototravel/Corbis

RIGHT: Rhodes—the largest of the Dodecanese islands—described as "more beautiful than the sun" by the ancient Greeks. Today, the island is still a tourist magnet due to its climate.
Letty/Fotolia

FAR RIGHT: Dating back to the 9th Century B.C., the majority of Ancient Thira that is visible today dates from 600 years when the Ptolemies used the port as their base.
vospalej/Fotolia

FAR LEFT: One of the most popular and visually breathtaking holiday destinations in Greece, the island of Santorini has proved to be a vast treasurehouse of archaeological data.
philipus/Fotolia

LEFT: With its volcanic geological structure, Santorini also boasts some fascinating natural phenomena.
Albo/Fotolia

FAR LEFT: The capital of the Ionian islands, Corfu town provides an attractive alternative to lazing on the sand.
Martyn Osman/fotoLibra

LEFT: Oia, on the island of Santorini, is famous for its fabulous sunsets. Locals claim that the fishing docks are the oldest continually used docks in the world, having been in service for 3,000 years.
philipus/Fotolia

RIGHT: The main town on the island of Symi has the same name, however it is more commonly known as Yialos. Part of the Dodecanese chain, the island boasts numerous isolated coves.
via Jo St. Mart

FAR RIGHT: The picturesque hamlet of Assos on Kefalonia. Many of the buildings on the island were damaged by an earthquake in 1953 but the area has since been rebuilt.
Keith Erskine/fotoLibra

FAR LEFT: The harbor at Aegina (one of the Islands in the Sarconic Gulf) is teeming with merchants selling their wares, be it octopii fresh from the ocean or fruit and vegetables.
via Jo St. Mart

LEFT: Another Sarconic Island, Hydra has long attracted visitors, as demonstrated by the cruise ship entering the harbor.
via Jo St. Mart

OVER PAGE: Acrocorinth is a monolithic rock overseeing the ancient city of Corinth and was continuously occupied from archaic times to the early 19th Century.
B N O'Donovan/fotoLibra

Hills and Mountains

Hills and Mountains

Considering its size and somewhat barren topography, it seems surprising that Greece could have had such a profound and lasting effect on the modern world. It is a difficult country to traverse with over four fifths of the mainland being mountainous or hill country, including the illustrious Mount Olympus. The highest point, Mytikas, ascends to an impressive 2,917 meters, so perhaps it is unsurprising that the followers of the ancient gods believed this to be seat of Zeus himself. No now longer considered a holy place, it has become a popular destination for hikers rather than priests.

The Pindus mountain range, often called "the spine of Greece" as it winds its way along the border of Thessaly and Epirus, stretches from the north of the country all the way to southern Albania. The highest point of the Pindus is Mount Smolikas; measuring 2,637 meters it is the second highest mountain in Greece.

Mount Athos, or "Holy Mountain" as it is also known, is dotted with twenty monasteries and has been declared a World Heritage Site as well as an autonomous monastic state. According to Greek mythology, Poseidon defeated one of the Titans, sworn enemies of the gods, and buried him under the mountain. Mount Athos also has strong ties to Christianity as stories tell of the Virgin Mary visiting this spot while sailing from Joppa to Cyprus. Somewhat ironically, these days females of any kind, including animals, are no longer allowed in the area by order of the monks. There is evidence that following the death of Alexander the Great in 323 B.C., Dinocrates the architect planned to carve the whole mountain into a likeness of the fallen ruler. Had he succeeded, we would not have the chance to admire the natural, breath-taking beauty of this location.

RIGHT AND FAR RIGHT: Lasithi Plateau on Crete provides a rich area for cultivation. It's main claim to fame, however, is the birthplace of Zeus.
Jonathan Peter Gray/fotoLibra and Stephen Mcadam/fotoLibra

FAR LEFT: The world's deepest gorge, Vikos Gorge in Zagorohoria, runs from Monodendri in the south to the Papingo villages in the north and is 900m at its deepest.
David Walton/fotoLibra

LEFT: The Kallergi mountain refuge is located above the plateau of Omalos and the gorge of Samaria on Crete.
Julia Dianne Jones/fotoLibra

OVER PAGE: Nestling in Western Greece, the village of Andritsena overlooks the valley of the River Alfios.
Andreas G. Karelias/fotoLibra

LEFT AND FAR LEFT: Research suggests that the pinnacles of the Meteora were formed around 60 million years ago. Weathering and earthquakes have since been responsible for their present shape.
*Andrew Buckin/Fotolia and
Ivo Velinov/Fotolia*

FAR LEFT: Considered to be one of the wildest gorges in Crete and one of the most difficult to cross, Ha Gorge is located in the plain of Ierapetra on the west slope of Thrypti mountain.
Stephen Mcadam/fotoLibra

LEFT: The mountainous regions of Greece can make driving seem perilous. Here, cars negotiate switchbacks to climb Vikos Gorge.
Paul A. Souders/Corbis

FAR LEFT: A spectacular sunset at Mount Athos. It is home to a semi-autonomous monastic republic that follows the Julian calendar and entrance is strictly limited to 10 non-Orthodox and 100 Orthodox adult males per day.
Roy Pedersen/fotoLibra

LEFT: The view above the Samaria Gorge, a national park in Crete. The gorge was created by a small river running between the White Mountains and Mount Volakias.
Ute & Juergen Schimmelpfennig/zefa/Corbis

FAR LEFT: The Samaria Gorge is 16 kilometers long, starts at an altitude of 1,250m at the northern entrance and ends at the shores of the Libyan Sea in Agia Roumeli.
Walter Bibikow/Corbis

LEFT: The highest mountain in Greece at 2,919m, Mount Olympus is noted for its rich flora with several endemic species and has long been regarded as the "home of the gods."
Walter Bibikow/JAI/Corbis

OVER PAGE: Lake Kournas—Crete's only lake—allegedly used to be full of eels but is now better known for its terrapins and tourism. There are rumours of a lost city submerged beneath its waters but no trace has ever been found.
Paul Cowan/Fotolia

Rivers, Lakes and Waterways

Rivers, Lakes and Waterways

The ancient Greeks were masters of the seas, but the waterways, lakes and rivers of Greece have also played a vital role in the workings of the country down through the centuries. Today, the country has about 37 lakes, both natural and man-made, including the large Lake Volvi and Lake Kerkini.

Lake Kerkini, an artificial reservoir built in 1932 on what was originally marshland, is now one of the foremost sites for bird watching in the country. Thanks to the rich soil—which nurtures large numbers of aquatic plants that in turn mean plentiful fish—plus its protected location, the lake is home to thousands of rare birds, amphibians, reptiles, and even a herd of buffalo.

The second largest lake in Greece, Lake Volvi is not far from Lake Kerkini and covers an area of just over 42 square miles. It is thought that in prehistoric times, the lake and marshlands completely covered the ancient Mygdonia region of Greece (now known as Thrace). Both are linked to the Strymon River, a massive waterway some 258 miles long that begins at Vitosha Mountain of Bulgaria and flows in to the Aegean Sea, near Amphipolis. A legend of this mighty river tells how in 480 B.C., Xerxes I of Persia was marching his army to Greece, his mind set on conquest. He came across the River Strymon and feared the river god would try to hinder him in his quest. In the finest tradition of the ancient kings, Xerxes decided a sacrifice would appease any angry god and had nine young boys and nine virgin girls buried alive near the waters edge. He passed over the river safely but would eventually be defeated and killed by Alexander I of Macedon in 479 B.C., just by the estuary of the Strymon River. It would seem that the river god had not been pleased with his sacrifice after all.

RIGHT: Melissani Lake, northwest of Sami, was rediscovered in 1951. In Greek mythology, Melissani was the cave of the nymphs.
Sheradon Dublin/fotoLibra

FAR RIGHT: A traditional Greek fisherman's house with the town of Messalonghi in the distance.
Nektarios Markogiannis/fotoLibra

ABOVE: The Rio–Antirio Bridge crosses the Gulf of Cornith near Patras and links the Peloponnese to mainland Greece. Officially it is called the Charilaos Trikloupis Bridge after the 19th Century Greek prime minister whose inspiration it was; the bridge, however, was not built until the 21st Century.
via Jo St. Mart

RIGHT: The Rio–Antirio Bridge looks even more impressive when illuminated.
Irineos Maliaris/Fotolia

LEFT AND RIGHT: The Aegean Sea lies between the mainland masses of Greece and Turkey and is important for shipping. It is also renowned for the disproportionately large number of islands it contains compared to other seas—such as Lemnos (left, the capital Myrina illustrated), strategically sited and the scene of two major naval battles: the Russian victory against the Turks in 1807 and Greek victory in 1913 during the Balkan Wars.
via Jo St. Mart

FAR LEFT: A boat in the Corinth Canal. The canal connects the Saronic Gulf with the Aegean Sea, cutting off the 250-mile journey around the Isthmus of Corinth. This amazing feat of engineering was achieved between 1881 and 1893. It is 69 feet wide and 26 feet deep at low tide, and gives passage to around 11,000 ships a year.
Mikey/Fotolia

LEFT: The Gulf of Cornith separates the Peloponnese from western mainland Greece and is one of the most seismically active regions in Europe.
via Jo St. Mart

LEFT: The Kalogeriko (or Plakida) triple-arch stone bridge near Kipi, Zagoria, was built in 1814. It is a perfect example of the art of the stone artisans of Epirus which the locals often call "a caterpillar in motion."
Tony Gervis/Robert Harding World Imagery/Corbis

RIGHT: One of the more popular treks on Crete is through the Sarakina Gorge where you will find this ancient Roman bridge traversing the river near the village of Mirtos.
Walter Bibikow/Corbis

GREECE

RIGHT: An infinity pool at sunrise overlooking the mountains of Albania taken from Ayios Stefanos, Corfu. *Ellen Rooney/Robert Harding World Imagery/Corbis*

FAR LEFT: Tables and chairs outside a cafe are covered in ice at Pamvotida Lake, in the city of Ioannina, February 2008. Heavy snow fell all over Greece, cutting access to villages and causing problems on the national highways while the temperatures reached minus 15 degrees Celsius in northern Greece.
Paraskevi Pappa/epa/Corbis

LEFT: A picturesque scene with a man-made waterway running through Alykes. Many of the buildings in this municipality on the island of Zakynthos were damaged during the Second World War and the Greek Civil War.
ambageo/Fotolia

OVER PAGE: Athens as seen from the Acropolis. The city is one of the oldest in the world and is often referred to as the cradle of Western civilization and the birthplace of democracy.
Paul A. Souders/Corbis

Towns and Cities

Towns and Cities

There are few places in the world that can rival Greece when it comes to vibrant, modern cities alongside buildings and monuments dating back millennia. Even fewer could compete with the nations capital, Athens. One of the oldest cities in the world, Athens has a recorded history dating back at least 3,400 years but archaeological evidence shows that there have been human settlements in the area for at least 4,500 years. Today Athens covers an area of 15 square miles (39 square kilometers) and has a population of nearly eight million. It was recently ranked the 32nd richest country in the world and has become a flourishing center for business. The Athens of Ancient Greece was an important focal point for the arts, learning, and philosophy. The eminent philosophers Aristotle and Plato both established academies in the city and their teacher, perhaps one of the greatest thinkers of all time, Socrates, was born in Athens. Remnants of the capital's mighty past are still evident throughout the city. Ancient monuments and sculptures still adorn the once powerful city-state, perhaps the most famous being the Parthenon, the temple dedicated to the goddess Athena.

Greece's second largest city and the capital of Macedonia is Thessaloniki. Originally established by King Cassander of Macedon in 315 B.C., he named the city after his wife, Thessalonike—the half sister of Alexander the Great. Nowadays the city is a major transportation hub, serving most of Greece and much of southeast Europe. The city also hosts many important events, such as an International Trade Fair and the Thessaloniki International Film Festival.

RIGHT: Iraklio (Heraklion) is Greece's fifth largest city and houses around a third of Crete's population. This is significantly boosted by the number of tourists who visit every year.
Stephen Mcadam/fotoLibra

RIGHT: The Athens Coastal Tram goes from Syntagma Square to the beaches of Glyfada and Voula. Many residents missed the city's previous tram system and were relieved when the authotiries instigated a new network in time for the 2004 Olympic Games.
Paul Mcnamara/Fotolia

FAR RIGHT: The National Archeaological Museum in Athens houses five large permanent collections: The Prehistoric Collection; The Sculptures Collection; The Vase and Minor Objects Collection; The Metallurgy Collection; and The Egyptian and Near Eastern Antiquities Collection.
Wolfgang Kaehler/Corbis

FAR LEFT: The first national parliament of the independent Greek state was only established in 1843, the same year that its current building was completed. It originally served as a palace for the Greek royal family until a referendum abolished the monarchy in 1924 and five years later the government decided to relocate from Old Parliament House.
via Jo St. Mart

LEFT: The Athens Metropolitan Area consists of 73 densely populated municipalities, sprawling around the city in virtually all directions. Not surprising as it is one of the world's oldest cities with a recorded history that spans around 3,400 years.
DeVIce/Fotolia

OVER PAGE: The spectacle that is Athens. The capital of modern Greece has had a checkered past since it first came to prominence in the 6th Century B.C.
James Hannibal/Fotolia

RIGHT: Athens at dusk—the Parthenon obvious at center right and beyond it the Saronic Gulf. At right is the port of Piraeus. *Pete Saloutos/zefa/Corbis*

FAR LEFT: The town hall of Kavala, the principal seaport of eastern Macedonia. The city was founded by settlers from Thasos in about the 6th Century B.C., who called it Neapolis ("new city").
Rainer Hackenberg/zefa/Corbis

LEFT: After the Greco-Turkish War of 1919, Kavala entered a new era of prosperity because of the labor offered by the thousands of refugees that moved to the area from Asia Minor.
Panos/Fotolia

FAR LEFT: From as early as the 16th Century, the windmills of The Hora have been one of the most recognized landmarks of Mykonos.
Marco Simoni/Robert Harding World Imagery/Corbis

LEFT: Hydra Port consists of a crescent-shaped harbor, around which is centered a strand of restaurants, shops and markets, all of which cater to tourists and locals (Hydriots).
via Jo St. Mart

OVER PAGE: Ippokratous Square in the Old Town of Rhodes surrounds a modest Castellania fountain, and is popular with tourists for its plethora of coffee shops and restaurants.
Atlantide Phototravel/Corbis

RIGHT: The Governor's Palace in Rhodes combines Byzantine, medieval and Spanish architectural styles.
Jeremy Horner/Corbis

FAR RIGHT: The Palace of the Grand Masters and Mandraki Harbor in Rhodes Town. The palace was built in the 14th Century by the Knights of Rhodes who occupied Rhodes from 1309 to 1522 although much of the original building was destroyed by an ammunition explosion in 1856.
Walter Bibikow/Corbis

FAR LEFT: A view over the city of Patras, from its old fortress, showing the dome of St. Andrew's Basilica.
Rachel Royse/Corbis

LEFT: Both Aristoteleous Street and Aristoteleous Square were named after the philosopher Aristotle and dominate the center of in Thessaloniki.
Walter Bibikow/JAI/Corbis

OVER PAGE: Temple of Poseidon, Cape Sounion, on the Attica peninsula. Perched on a cliff almost 200 feet above the sea, the temple was built c. 440 B.C. In Greek mythology Poseidon was the god of the sea and of earthquakes, and was ranked second only in importance to Zeus.
Herbert Spichtinger/zefa/Corbis

Places of Worship

Places of Worship

Throughout the ages, Greece has worshipped many different gods and as a result there are numerous ancient temples, churches, and monasteries across the country. The pantheistic days of Ancient Greece meant there were many gods to revere and temples and shrines abounded. With the adoption of Christianity, several of the ancient temples were converted into Christian places of worship, while others were destroyed or have been lost to the passage of time. The most famous of all the remaining ancient temples is the Parthenon in Athens. Dedicated to the goddess Athena, it was completed in 432 B.C., but was later converted into a Christian temple in the sixth century.

Other important religious shrines include the Tholos of Theodorus, the Temple of Hephaestus, the Erechtheum, and Stavronikita Monastery on Mount Athos. The Erechtheum was built to honor Athena Polias and Poseidon Erechtheus. The south side of the edifice is adorned with statues representing six women (known as *caryatids*) whose graceful appearance belies their strength. Despite each woman acting as a supporting column, one of them was removed by Lord Elgin and shipped to England, where the caryatid was used to decorate his home. He later sold it to the British Museum. Legend has it that the mournful wails of the remaining caryatids can be heard echoing every night as they call out for their lost sister.

RIGHT: The Stavronikita Monastery is built on top of a promentory near the sea on the Athonite peninsula. The site was first used by Athonite monks in the 10th Century.
Chris Hellier//Corbis

FAR LEFT: Angarathos monastery is one of the oldest monasteries in Crete and is dedicated to the Dormition of the Virgin. It owes its name to the "angarathia" (a type of bush) under which the icon of the Virgin was found.
Stephen Mcadam/fotoLibra

LEFT: The oldest surviving monastery on Rhodes, Thari dates from the 9th Century and has some of the most amazing frescoes on the island.
David James/fotoLibra

OVER PAGE: It has not been confirmed when the monasteries of Meteora were established, but hermit monks were believed to be living among the caves and cutouts in the rocks as early as the 11th Century A.D.
Netfalls/Fotolia

131

FAR LEFT: Roussanou Monastery—Agia Varvaras Roussanou—on Mount Athos in Meteora was founded in 1545 by two devout brothers, Joasaph and Maximos, on the site of an earlier church. The monks pull supplies up from the valley below using rope and pulleys.
MedioImages/Corbis

LEFT: The six remaining monasteries at Meteora are all perched high on sandstone pinnacles in the Pindus Mountains at the northwestern edge of the Plain of Thessaly; at the end of the 15th Century there were 24 monasteries here, but most are long gone. The Great Meteoron Monastery—or Megalo Meteoro—is the principle monastery in the complex and sits on the highest peak. It was founded in the mid-14th Century by the monk Athanasius Koinovitis.
Rainer Hackenberg/zefa/Corbis

RIGHT: The 19th Century Cathedral of Ayios Minas is located in St Catherine's Square in Heraklion and sits next to its predecessor.
Walter Bibikow/Corbis

FAR RIGHT: It is believed that the Church of Panaghia Kapnikarea was built some time in the 11th Century and as such is one of the oldest in Athens.
Walter Bibikow/Corbis

RIGHT: Although construction of the Temple of Olympian Zeus in Athens began in the 6th Century B.C. it was not completed until the 2nd Century A.D., some 650 years after the project had begun.
via Jo St. Mart

FAR RIGHT: The Temple of Aphaia is located within a sanctuary complex dedicated to the goddess Aphaia on the island of Aegina.
via Jo St. Mart

FAR LEFT: Basilica of Agios Titos is undeniably one of the oldest and most important monuments of Christianity in Crete. It was the seat of the first bishops of the Cretan Church.
Walter Bibikow/JAI/Corbis

LEFT: The impressive Basilica of St. Andrew, martyred in the city of Patras (the European Capital of Culture for 2006). Construction began in 1908 with its inauguration being held in 1974.
Rachel Royse/Corbis

FAR LEFT: In 1989 the Archaeological site of Mystras—including the fortress, palace, churches, and monasteries—were named a UNESCO World Heritage Site.
Jean-Pierre Lescourret/Corbis

LEFT: Although the first church on this spot was originally constructed in the 4th Century A.D., the curent Church of St. Demetrius in Thessaloniki dates from 634 A.D.
Vanni Archive/Corbis

143

Ancient Greece

Ancient Greece

Greece has often been called "the cradle of Western civilization" and not without cause. The Ancient Greeks were the first to embrace democracy, while the philosophy, arts, and architecture have set an example to the western world that has endured for millennia. Obviously, time has taken its toll on the relics of this period in Greek history but some fine examples of Ancient Greece still remain to this day. The Parthenon and the Acropolis are popular stops for any tourists that visit the nation's capital, but these are not the only examples available. Others include the Theatre of Dionysus, the Stoa of Attalos, and the Sanctuary of Asklepios at Epidaurus.

The Theatre of Dionysus is an open-air theater situated at the base of the Acropolis in Athens. Thought to be the first stone open-air theater ever constructed, it had a capacity of 17,000 and was dedicated to the god of plays and wine, Dionysus. Some renovations have been made throughout the ages, including the addition of stone seating in the mid 4th Century. Evidence also suggests that Emperor Nero made some changes in 61 B.C., adding some distinctly Roman touches to the original designs.

Another fine example of Ancient Greek architecture is the Stoa of Attalos. It was constructed by King Attalos II, the ruler of Pergamon between 159 B.C. and 138 B.C.. The original building was larger and more impressive than any other buildings in Ancient Athens at the time. Unfortunately, the Stoa was destroyed in 267 A.D. and the ruins were incorporated into a fortified wall around the city. Thankfully, the building was completely restored during the 1950s and is now the Ancient Agora Museum.

RIGHT: An artist's impression of how the Acropolis in Athens would have looked in its heyday.
Bettmann/Corbis

FAR RIGHT: The Acropolis viewed from the northwest in the latter half of the 19th Century. *Library of Congress*

PREVIOUS PAGE: The Acropolis is a spectacular sight when illuminated against the night sky.
Jan Dusek/fotoLibra

RIGHT: Caryatids on the Porch of the Maidens. Properly called the Erechtheum, the temple is on the north side of the Acropolis in Athens. It was probably designed by the architect Mnesicles and built between 421 and 407 B.C.
Larry Lee Photography/Corbis

FAR RIGHT: The Acropolis in Athens is one of the best known ancient heritage sites in the world. Most of the buildings on the flat hilltop were built during the Golden Age of Athens (460–430 B.C.) when the great Pericles ruled the city.
Pete Saloutos/Corbis

ABOVE: The first floor of the new Acropolis Museum in Athens. The official opening was on June 20, 2009. Located some 300 yards away from the Acropolis, the museum is a modern building with glass walls and floors, where visitors could enjoy the antiquities from the ancient temples while looking at the Acropolis through the glass.
Liang Yeqian/XinHua/Xinhua Press/Corbis

FAR RIGHT: The Temple of Olympian Zeus, Athens—the effects of years of wind and chemical erosion.
Image Source/Corbis

FAR RIGHT: The Odeon of Herodes Atticus is a stone theatre structure located on the south slope of the Acropolis of Athens. Built in 161 A.D. by Herodes Atticus in memory of his wife, Aspasia Annia Regilla, it was originally a steep-sloped amphitheater with a three-storey stone front wall and a wooden roof.
Clement Cheah/Fotolia

RIGHT: The arena is today used for the *son et lumiere* of the Acropolis, which takes place on most summer evenings.
Clement Cheah/Fotolia

FAR LEFT: The Erechtheum was built entirely of marble from Mount Pentelikon, with friezes of black limestone from Eleusis which bore sculptures executed in relief in white marble.
via Jo St. Mart

LEFT: The people responsible for the construction of the Arch of Hadrian are forgotten in the mists of time but it did span an ancient road from the center of Athens to the complex of structures on the eastern side of the city that included the Temple of Olympian Zeus.
Library of Congress

RIGHT: The Theater at Delphi dates from the 4th Century B.C. and was built further up the hill from the Temple of Apollo, thereby giving spectators a view of the entire sanctuary and the valley below.
via Jo St. Mart

FAR RIGHT: Situated between Athens and Piraeus is the town of Kalithea, the site of these thermal baths. The town and its citizens are mentioned among other places in Plato's *Dialogues*.
Hubert Stadler/Corbis

RIGHT: The ruins at Knossos, the capital of Minoan Crete, were discovered in the early 19th Century. It was here that King Minos kept his mythical Minotaur.
Phil Jones/fotoLibra

FAR RIGHT: The ruins of the ancient city of Kamiros on Rhodes. Earthquakes in 226 B.C. and 142 B.C. destroyed the city.
Stephen Mcadam/fotoLibra

FAR LEFT: The Paestum Archeological Site with the Temple of Neptune in the background. There are the remains of three temples in this locale which were dedicated to Hera and Athena, although they have traditionally been identified as a basilica and temples of Neptune and Ceres, owing to 18th Century mis-attribution.
Mimmo Jodice/Corbis

LEFT: The interior of the Stoa of Attalos in Athens. It was built by and named after King Attalos II of Pergamon who ruled between 159 B.C. and 138 B.C.
Ruggero Vanni/Corbis

FAR LEFT: The Theater of Ancient Messene is believed to date from around the 1st to the 2nd Century B.C. The ancient city is situated at the foot of Mount Ithome, where settlement had already existed for around 600 years. *Vanni Archive/Corbis*

LEFT: A stone archway at Olympia, the site of the Olympic Games in classical times. Emperor Theodosius I abolished them in 394 A.D. as they were then considered reminiscent of paganism. *Pete Saloutos/zefa/Corbis*

OVER PAGE: The classical period, between the 5th and 4th centuries B.C., was the golden age of the site at Olympia. *Pete Saloutos/zefa/Corbis*

RIGHT: The Tholos at the sanctuary of Athena Pronaia in Delphi was a circular building constructed between 380 and 360 B.C. It consisted of 20 Doric columns, three of which have been restored.
Richard T. Nowitz/Corbis

FAR RIGHT: The Roman Forum in Thessaloniki was destroyed when an earthquake severely damaged the city in 620 A.D.
Jon Arnold/JAI/Corbis

FAR LEFT: A peacock climbs the steps to the ancient city of Ialissos that stood on Mount Filérimos on Rhodes. Here there are foundations of a 4th Century B.C. temple and a palaeo-Christian basilica.
Walter Bibikow/Corbis

LEFT: Cassope is considered the best preserved ancient Greek city today. It was destroyed by Roman forces in 177–176 B.C. and abandoned in 31 B.C.
René Mattes/Hemis/Corbis

OVER PAGE: The Battle of Lapiths and Centaurs from the Temple of Apollo at Bassae. The sculpture depicts the battle between the Centaurs and the Lapiths at the wedding of Pirithous and Hippodamia.
The Gallery Collection/Corbis

Art, Sculptures and Statues

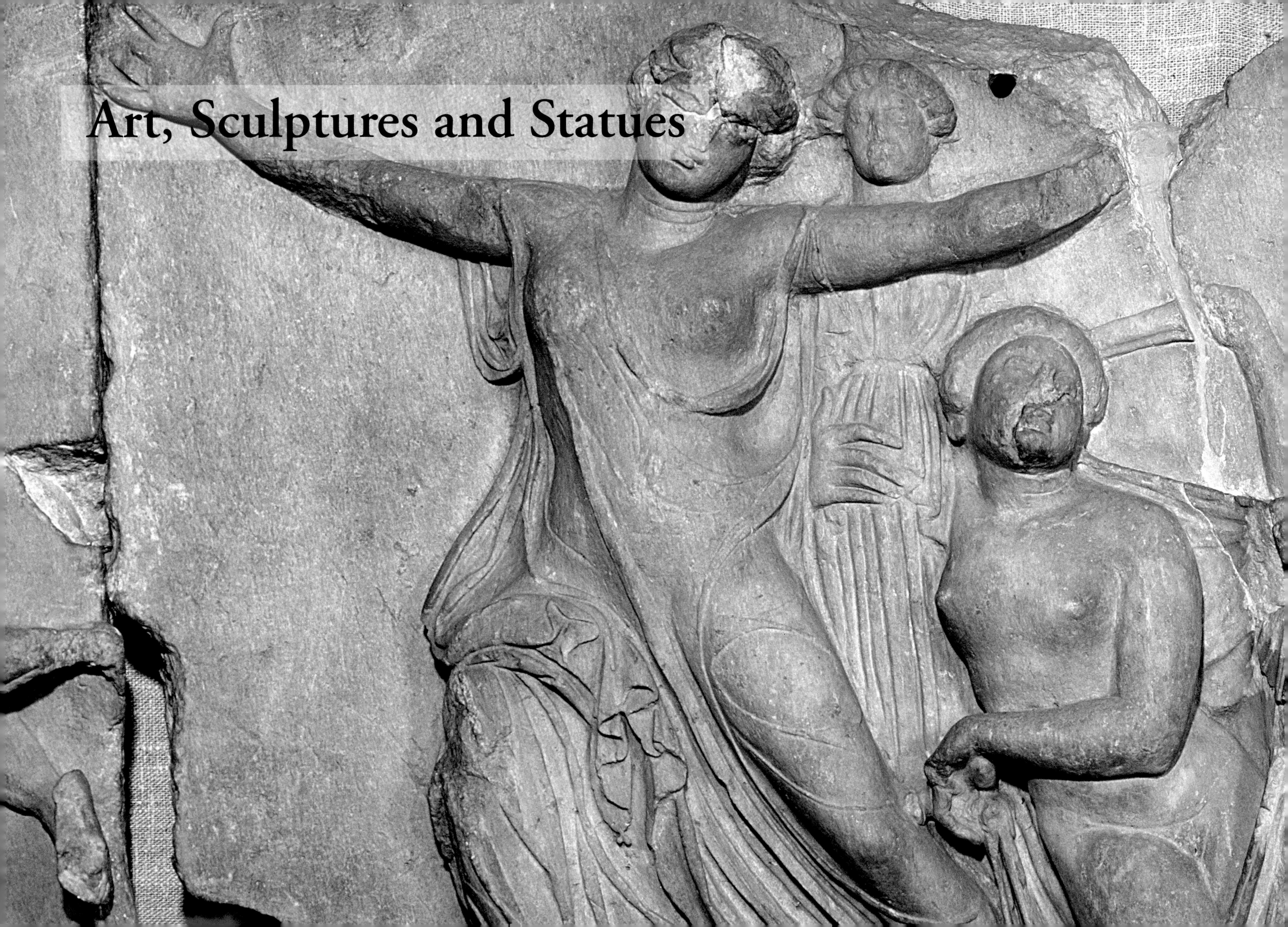

Art, Sculptures and Statues

Although we tend to think of Greek art in terms of "Classical" sculpture and beautiful symmetry, the artwork of Greece has undergone many changes, over the years incorporating aspects of the cultures that have occupied the country. For example, there are many fine examples of Byzantine mosaics which survive today and illustrate the influence of that great power on the artists of Greece. Ottoman influences are also apparent, as are Roman, Myceneaen, and on rare occasions even Minoan.

Due to the long periods of time involved, there are few remnants of ancient Greek art. The paintings of antiquity were completed on wooden tablets that, if kept properly, could last hundreds of years, though not thousands. The only remains of this time are usually in the more hardwearing forms of sculpture, pottery, or jewelry. One of the most famous sculptures that has managed to survive is the Charioteer of Delphi. This life-size bronze statue was originally one part of a much larger group that is thought to have included four or six horses, the chariot, two grooms, as well as the remaining charioteer. Initially erected at Delphi in 474 B.C., the sculpture celebrated the victory of the chariot team in the Pythian Games. When discovered in 1896, the statue was in three pieces, but has since been reassembled and remains in excellent condition despite the loss of the charioteer's left arm. It now resides in the Delphi Archaeological Museum.

RIGHT: Detail of one of the fascinating Minoan frescoes in the Palace of Knossos on Crete. One remarkable feature of their art is the color-coding of the sexes: the men are depicted with ruddy skin, the women as milky white.
Walter Bibikow/JAI/Corbis

FAR LEFT: The remains of a Roman statue presides in front of a Byzantine Church in Gortys, Crete. This was originally thought to represent the Emperor Antoninus Pius, but some argue that it is the statue of an unknown scholar or philosopher.
Phil Jones/fotoLibra

LEFT: These lions were originally sited to guard the Sanctuary of Apollo in his birthplace, Delos. Unearthed between 1886 and 1906, the statues have since been relocated to the Archaeological Museum of Delos to prevent further erosion.
Brigida Soriano/Fotolia

RIGHT: The statue of Cleobolus, one of the seven sages of antiquity, on Rhodes, with Lindos in the background.
Stephen Mcadam/fotoLibra

FAR RIGHT: The site of the ancient Temple of Zeus was identified in 1766 and excavation began in 1829 with a French team taking several fragments of the pediments to the Musée du Louvre. Here, The West Pediment shows Apollo intervening in the battle between Lapiths and Centaurs which flared up at the marriage of Theseus's friend Peirithoos with Deidameia.
Vanni Archive/Corbis

LEFT: The Siphnian Treasury at Delphi boasted the finest Archaic example of an Ionic frieze. The north side depicted a battle of gods against giants.
René Mattes/Hemis/Corbis

RIGHT: The West Pediment of the Archaic Temple of Artemis in Kerkira was excavated at Palaiopolis in the early 20th Century.
Vanni Archive/Corbis

FAR LEFT: An ancient Greek warrior boarding his chariot. These vehicles quickly became an important military tool and the earliest spoke-wheeled chariots date from around 2000 B.C.
Gianni Dagli Orti/Corbis

LEFT: The Diadumene Room in the National Archaeological Museum in Athens. The museum is the largest in the country and was originally set up to house excavated finds from 19th Century Athens but it now boasts more than 20,000 items from all around Greece.
Jean-Pierre Lescourret/Corbis

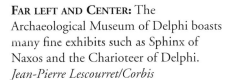

FAR LEFT: A Minoan depiction of a ship in a harbor in Santorini. This Bronze Age civilization thrived between 3000 to 2000 B.C., and reached its peak in the period 2000 to 1580 B.C.
Gianni Dagli Orti/Corbis

LEFT: A more recent addition to the arts in Greece is this sculpture of seagulls on the path to Rhodes town.
Stephen Mcadam/fotoLibra

ABOVE: The National Gallery in Athens was established in 1878 and is devoted to modern Greek and European art from the 14th Century to the 20th Century.
Amet Jean Pierre/Corbis Sygma

RIGHT: A statue of Atenea—also known as Athena, Greek goddess of wisdom, household arts and crafts, spinning and weaving, textiles—in Athens. Legend has it that Athena sprang fully-grown and fully-armed from the head of her father, Zeus, ruler of the gods on Mount Olympus.
Brigida Soriano/Fotolia

FAR RIGHT: Statues of Plato and Socrates sit thoughtfully outside the Academy of Athens. They were sculpted out of marble from the mountain of Penteli by Italian sculptor Piccarelli and placed in their present location in 1885.
Brigida Soriano/Fotolia

FAR LEFT: *The School of Athens* by Raphael was painted between 1510–11 in the Apostolic Palace in the Vatican. While the identity of many of the subjects are open to debate, in the center are the two undisputed main subjects: Plato on the left and Aristotle, his student, on the right.
The Gallery Collection/Corbis

LEFT: Statues of Apollo and Socrates in Athens. Socrates was a Classical Greek philosopher who lived between 469 B.C.–399 B.C.
Brigida Soriano/Fotolia

OVER PAGE: People relaxing outside shops in Paleohori, on the Greek island of Lesbos.
Macduff Everton/Corbis

Living in Greece

Living in Greece

Each year Greece welcomes nearly twenty million visitors to its shores and has been designated one of the top ten tourist destinations in the world. Given the beautiful scenery, wealth of historic landmarks, and gorgeous coastal towns surrounded by sandy beaches and crystal clear waters, it is not surprising so many people come to get a taste for life in Greece.

It is possible to enjoy a more literal taste of the country by sampling the local cuisine. The Greek diet is often cited as one of the healthiest in Europe, with most of the national dishes using fresh ingredients and olive oil in almost every recipe. Some of the most popular are *moussaka*, Greek salad, and *souvlaki*. Dishes often change from region to region, especially when it comes to herbs and spices. For example, to the north of the mainland it is much more common to use sweet spices, such as cinnamon or cloves, when cooking meat dishes. Some of the local meals can even be traced all the way back to ancient Greece. For example, *skordalia* (a melange of walnuts, olive oil, garlic, and almonds) has been served here for 2,000 years.

Greece is also one of the few remaining European countries that still has compulsory military service for young men. Each male aged between 18 and 45 (females are exempt) must serve at least 12 months in the military, although recently the government has promised to abolish this particular aspect of Greek life.

RIGHT: This taverna could be anywhere in Greece, such is the popularity of these establishments. Tourists and residents alike enjoy stopping for refreshments and watching the world go by.
Ragne Kabanova/Fotolia

FAR RIGHT: A familiar sight in rural Greece where inhabitants rely on a more traditional mode of transport.
Keith Erskine/fotoLibra

RIGHT AND FAR RIGHT: With seafood so popular on restaurant menus, fishing, in all its guises, is an important vocation in many parts of Greece.
Jan Holm/fotoLibra and Keith Erskine/fotoLibra

FAR LEFT: Members of the elite Evzones light infantry unit provide a 24-hour honor guard, with an hourly guard change, at the Presidential Mansion and at the Tomb of the Unknown Soldier in Athens. The ceremony has become a big hit with tourists.
M&n/fotoLibra

LEFT: A small market below the Cathedral of Panaghia provides an ideal opportunity for tourists to sample the local fayre.
Martyn Osman/fotoLibra

RIGHT: Olives, pickled vegetables, Greek anise-flavored Ouzo and a few international alcohols and colas, on offer at an outdoor market in Iraklion.
Gail Mooney/Corbis

FAR RIGHT: Cheese is an extremely popular food in Greece although many varieties—other than feta—are not widely known outside the country.
Rainer Hackenberg/zefa/Corbis

LEFT AND FAR LEFT: Two traditional Greek dishes: a mezze (a selection of small dishes, hot or cold, spicy or savory) and a Greek salad (typically made of sliced or chopped tomatoes with slices of cucumber, red onion, feta cheese and kalamata olives, seasoned with salt, black pepper, oregano, and basil and dressed with olive oil).
Ludovic Maisant/Corbis and Owen Franken/Corbis

RIGHT: Octopus is a common food in Mediterranean cuisine—three specimens are pictured here drying in sun. Care must be taken to boil the octopus properly, to ensure that any slime and the smell, as well as any residual ink, are removed. *Eliott Slater/Hemis/Corbis*

FAR RIGHT: Tourists relax at a restaurant in Chania Harbor at sunset. The resort is located on the north coast of Crete and its picturesque scenery is the perfect setting for such a moment.
Atlantide Phototravel/Corbis

FAR LEFT: Greece is one of the oldest wine-producing regions in the world with evidence suggesting that the industry is more than 6,500 years old. Here, a farmer sprays his wine fields in Thessaloniki. *Stefania Mizara/Corbis*

LEFT: The culmination of hard work and expertise: the wine maker pours a glass of red wine for wine tasters at Embonas in Rhodes. *Gail Mooney/Corbis*

RIGHT: Such is the importance of agriculture that farmers are prepared to make their voices heard when necessary. Hundreds of tractors blocked the road near Larissa city, central Greece, on January 29, 2009 protesting against the government's farm policy.
Vassiliki Paschali/epa/Corbis

FAR RIGHT: A herd of cows cross the Titarisios River, Larissa, in March 2009. Recent heavy rains in the Thessaly Plain raised the water level in the river to near overflow proportions.
Vassiliki Paschali/epa/Corbis

OVER PAGE: The 75,000-capacity Olympic Stadium in Athens during renovations in preparation for the 2004 Summer Olympics.
Paul A Souders/Corbis

Sports

Naturally for the country that invented the Olympic Games, sports of all kinds have always been popular. The first modern Olympic Games were hosted here in 1896 at the Panathinaiko stadium in Athens (the only stadium in the world built entirely with white marble). Greece also claims many successful football teams. Some sixteen make up the Greek Super League, running from August to May each year, every team play thirty games each. The most successful of these are Olympiacos, Panathinaikos, and AEK Athens—often referred to as the "Big Three." The national team is positioned twentieth in the world and gained a surprise victory in the 2004 UEFA European Championships.

However, football is not the only game that attracts an avid following in this country. Water polo, windsurfing, and scuba diving are also very popular. For those who enjoy a more extreme (and much louder) form of entertainment, the Acropolis Rally is held on the outskirts of the Athens every year. Taking place at the hottest time of the year, drivers undergo a gruelling test of skill and endurance as they hurtle their way through the dusty mountainous roads around the city. With temperatures occasionally reaching as high as fifty degrees celsius and with the mixture of difficult terrain and suffocating dust, this is classed as one of the most arduous rallies in the world.

The Acropolis Rally was awarded the coveted title of Rally of the Year in 2005.

RIGHT: Fiery Olympic rings atop a lake of water in the middle of the Athens Olympic stadium during the opening ceremony of the 2004 Olympic Games.
Rolf Kosecki/Corbis

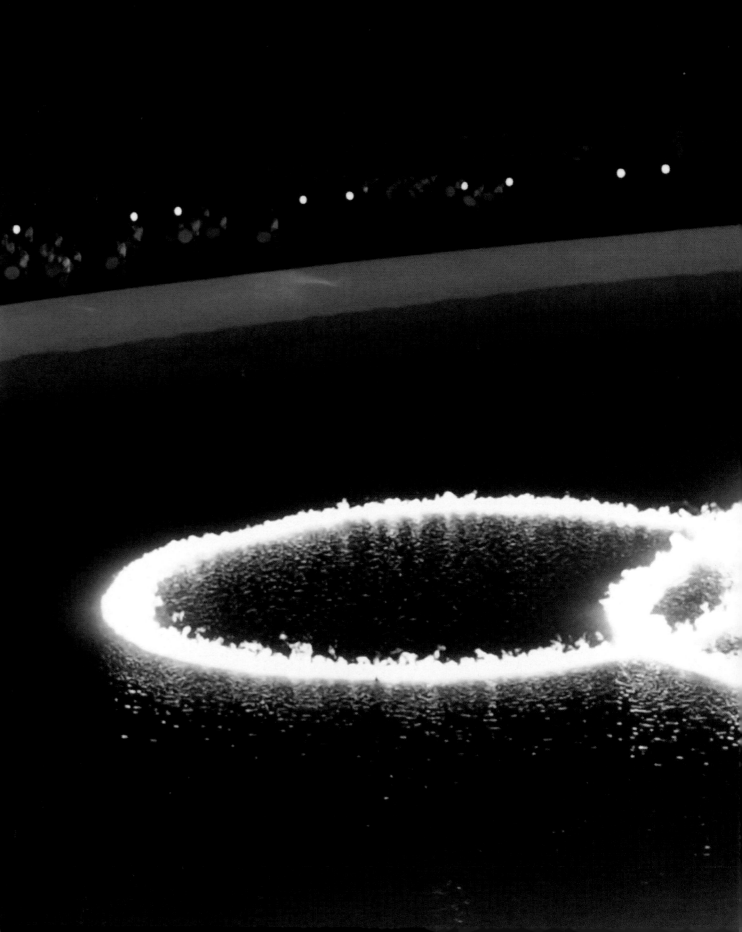

LEFT: The Panatheniac Stadium was built to host the first modern Olympic Games in 1896. Nine sporting disciplines—athletics, cycling, fencing, gymnastics, shooting, swimming, tennis, weightlifting and wrestling—were featured. The rowing events had to be cancelled due to bad weather conditions.
AnneCatherine Mittey/Fotolia

FAR LEFT: Women compete in the Mistral class of windsurfing during the Athens 2002 Regatta off the coast of Pireas. This was the sailing venue for the 2004 Athens Olympics. Women were not initially allowed to participate in the modern Olympics until they were first invited to compete in 1928.
Andreas Neumeier/NewSport/Corbis

LEFT: Cyclists pass Hadrian's Arch during the men's Olympic road race in August 2004. Some 144 competitors participated in the 17 lap race through central Athens.
Laurent Rebours/Pool/Reuters/Corbis

RIGHT: An aerial view of the Athens Olympic stadium during the first super special stage of the Acropolis rally of Greece in 2005. The 52nd Acropolis rally, for the World Rally Championship (WRC) started in the Olympic stadium packed with more than 65,000 spectators. *Yannis Behrakis/Reuters/Corbis*

FAR RIGHT: A more traditional rallying image as Carlos Sainz and Marc Marti compete in their Citroen Xsara during the Acropolis 2005 WRC Rally. *Jo Lillini/Corbis*

RIGHT AND FAR RIGHT: Water sports are very popular all around Greece with scuba diving and kite surfing in particular being very common activities.
Roy Bjarne Pedersen/fotoLibra and Kai Koehler/Fotolia

RIGHT: Giorgos Karagounis and captain Theodoros Zagorakis run with the trophy after beating hosts Portugal in July 2004. The unfancied Greek national football side pulled off an amazing coup when they won the Euro 2004 championship. *Kai Pfaffenbach/Reuters/Corbis*

FAR RIGHT: Greek football fans are passionate about their team. Here the sorrow of defeat is etched on the painted face of a Greek supporter watching his team lose 0–1 to Russia and suffer elimination from Euro 2008. *Matthew Ashton/AMA/Corbis*

Index